ELECTRICITY

AT

WORK

REBECCA FELIX

Consulting Editor, Diane Craig, M.A./Reading Specialist

Sandcastle

An Imprint of Abdo Publishing
abdopublishing.com

abdopublishing.com

Published by Abdo Publishing, a division of ABDO, PO Box 398166, Minneapolis, Minnesota 55439. Copyright © 2017 by Abdo Consulting Group, Inc. International copyrights reserved in all countries. No part of this book may be reproduced in any form without written permission from the publisher. SandCastle™ is a trademark and logo of Abdo Publishing.

Printed in the United States of America, North Mankato, Minnesota

062016
092016

THIS BOOK CONTAINS
RECYCLED MATERIALS

Design: Mighty Media, Inc.
Content Developer: Nancy Tuminelly
Production: Mighty Media, Inc.
Editor: Liz Salzmann
Photo Credits: Shutterstock, Wikimedia Commons

Library of Congress Cataloging-in-Publication Data

Names: Felix, Rebecca, 1984- author.
Title: Electricity at work / Rebecca Felix ; consulting editor, Diane Craig, M.A./reading specialist.
Description: Minneapolis, Minnesota : Abdo Publishing, [2017] | Series: Science at work
Identifiers: LCCN 2015050527 (print) | LCCN 2016000127 (ebook) | ISBN 9781680781397 (print) | ISBN 9781680775822 (ebook)
Subjects: LCSH: Electricity--Juvenile literature.
Classification: LCC QC527.2 .F45 2017 (print) | LCC QC527.2 (ebook) | DDC 537--dc23
LC record available at http://lccn.loc.gov/2015050527

SandCastle™ Level: Fluent

SandCastle™ books are created by a team of professional educators, reading specialists, and content developers around five essential components—phonemic awareness, phonics, vocabulary, text comprehension, and fluency—to assist young readers as they develop reading skills and strategies and increase their general knowledge. All books are written, reviewed, and leveled for guided reading, early reading intervention, and Accelerated Reader™ programs for use in shared, guided, and independent reading and writing activities to support a balanced approach to literacy instruction. The SandCastle™ series has four levels that correspond to early literacy development. The levels are provided to help teachers and parents select appropriate books for young readers.

EMERGING · BEGINNING · TRANSITIONAL · FLUENT

CONTENTS

ABOUT ELECTRICITY

Do you watch TV? Do you use a **tablet**? Have you ever turned on the lights?

Then you
have used
electricity!

Electricity is a form of **energy**.
It can come from nature.

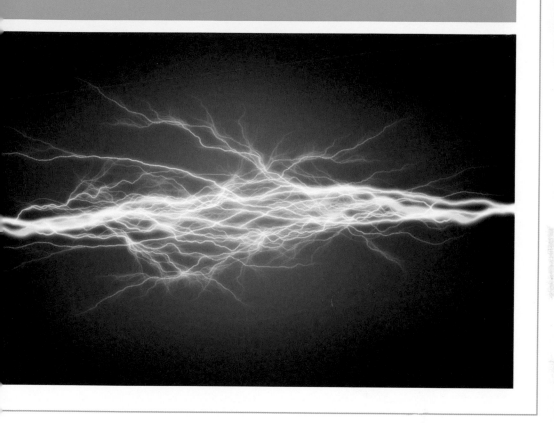

Lightning is a burst of electricity.

Many scientists study electricity.
Benjamin Franklin was one.

He experimented
with lightning.

Electricity can be man-made too.
It is made in **power plants**.

Wires carry electricity to buildings.
Then people can use it.

Dax uses an electric lamp.

It has a **cord**. It **plugs** into a **socket**.

Sam dries her hair.

She uses an electric dryer.
It also **plugs** in.

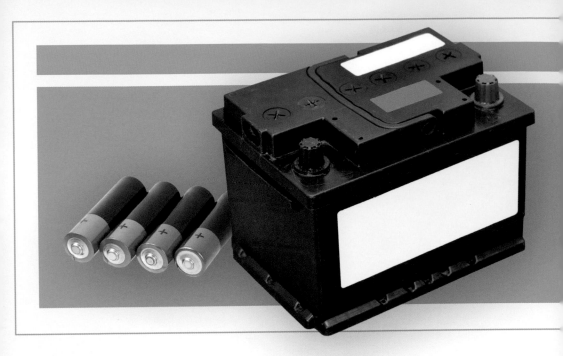

Batteries store electricity.
They come in many sizes.

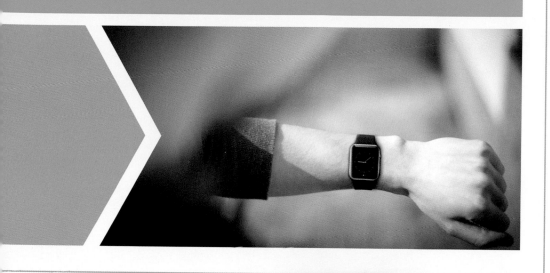

They power
wireless things.

17

Abe and Lynn go camping.

They have lights on their hats.
The lights use batteries.

Anna's class uses **tablets**.

Tablets have
batteries too.

THINK ABOUT IT

Look around you!
Where else is electricity at work?

How do
you use it?

GLOSSARY

cord – a wrapped electrical wire used to connect things to a power source.

energy – a natural power that can affect other things.

plug – to stick the end of a cord into an outlet or other hole.

power plant – a factory that makes electricity.

socket – an opening that holds something, such as a light socket.

tablet – a small, flat computer.